BEST PRACTICES in Action

Nonfiction Read & Write Booklets
Holidays

by Alyse Sweeney

NEW YORK • TORONTO • LONDON • AUCKLAND • SYDNEY
MEXICO CITY • NEW DELHI • HONG KONG • BUENOS AIRES

Teaching Resources

For Ginnie

Cover design by Brian LaRossa

Cover and interior illustrations by Maxie Chambliss

Interior design by Ellen Matlach for Boultinghouse & Boultinghouse, Inc.

ISBN-13: 978-0-439-56758-9

ISBN-10: 0-439-56758-0

Copyright © 2007 by Alyse Sweeney

Published by Scholastic Inc.

All rights reserved.

Printed in the U.S.A.

1 2 3 4 5 6 7 8 9 10   40   15 14 13 12 11 10 09 08 07

Contents

Nonfiction Read & Write Booklets

Introduction

During the time I was a Scholastic editor, a large part of my job was finding out from primary-grade teachers what materials would be most useful to them in the classroom. Over the years second- and third-grade teachers spoke of the growing need for the following:

- engaging nonfiction texts that tie in to the curriculum
- more opportunities to engage students in meaningful writing
- writing prompts that connect to texts and build higher-order thinking skills

Nonfiction Read & Write Booklets: Holidays delivers each of these valuable components in an interactive mini-book format. The ten booklets cover key topics about holidays and engage students with lively text, thought-provoking writing prompts, and opportunities to draw. Best of all, when students are finished, they'll have a unique, personalized book to take home and share. The sense of ownership and accomplishment that comes with completing these mini-books is highly motivating.

Each booklet is filled with a variety of nonfiction features and structures to help students learn to navigate informational text. They'll learn key concepts from reading charts, webs, and diagrams. In addition, each mini-book presents students with opportunities to write informational text. After reading a chart, diagram, or short passage, students are asked to infer, evaluate, apply, analyze, compare, explain, or summarize. As a result, children develop critical-thinking skills and gain a deeper understanding of each topic.

With these interactive booklets in hand, children reflect upon what they are reading, think critically, develop their own ideas, and express themselves in writing. Nonfiction Read & Write Booklets provide an engaging format for helping students comprehend the features of nonfiction and for satisfying their curiosity about the world around them.

Why Teach Nonfiction?

Research has provided insight into the importance of teaching nonfiction. Here are some key findings:

- Informational text helps students build knowledge of the world around them (e.g., Anderson & Guthrie, 1999; Duke & Kays, 1998, as cited in Duke & Bennett-Armistead, 2003). This can potentially deepen students' comprehension of subsequent texts (e.g., Wilson & Anderson, 1986, as cited in Duke & Bennett-Armistead, 2003).

- Many students struggle with content area reading (Vacca, 2002; Walpole, 1998, as cited in Kristo and Bamford, 2004). Providing students with high-quality nonfiction materials may help better prepare them to meet these challenges.

- Providing students in the lower grades with more exposure to nonfiction may alleviate the decline in achievement often observed in fourth grade (Chall, Jacobs, and Baldwin, 1990; Duke, 2000, as cited in Boynton and Blevins, 2005).

- Exposing students in the early grades to informational texts helps improve their skills as readers and writers of informational text when they are older (Papps, 1991; Sanacore, 1991, as cited in Kristo and Bamford, 2004).

- Studies have shown that some students prefer nonfiction to fiction (Donovan, Smolkin, and Lomax, 2000; Caswell and Duke, 1998, as cited in Boynton and Blevins, 2004). Including more nonfiction materials in your classroom instruction taps into these students' interests and may increase their level of motivation.

- Teaching students to read nonfiction will give them real-world skills and prepare them for the materials they'll read outside of school. One study found that the text on the World Wide Web is 96 percent expository (Kamil & Lane, 1998, as cited in Duke & Bennett-Armistead, 2003). Students will encounter informational text not only on the Web but also all around them—it's essential that they have the tools to comprehend it.

Connections to the Standards

These books are designed to support you in meeting the following standards outlined by Mid-continent Research for Education and Learning (McREL), an organization that collects and synthesizes national and state standards.

Reading

—Uses the general skills and strategies of the reading process, including:

- Uses meaning clues such as picture captions, title, cover, and headings to aid comprehension.

—Uses reading skills and strategies to understand and interpret a variety of informational texts, including:

- Understands the main idea and supporting details of simple expository information.
- Relates new information to prior knowledge and experience.
- Uses text organizers (e.g., headings, topic and summary sentences, graphic features, typeface) to determine the main ideas and to locate information in a text.
- Understands structural patterns or organization in informational texts (e.g., chronological, logical, or sequential order; compare-and-contrast; cause-and-effect; proposition and support).

Writing

—Uses the general skills and strategies of the writing process.

—Uses the stylistic and rhetorical aspects of writing.

—Uses grammatical and mechanical conventions in written compositions.

History

—Understands selected attributes and historical developments of societies in Africa, the Americas, Asia, and Europe.

- Knows the holidays and ceremonies of different societies.

—Understands how democratic values came to be, and how they have been exemplified by people, events, and symbols.

- Understands how important figures reacted to their times and why they were significant to the history of our democracy.
- Understands the historical events and democratic values commemorated by major national holidays.

Civics

—Understands the central ideas of American constitutional government and how this form of government has shaped the character of American society.

—Understands the importance of Americans' sharing and supporting certain values, beliefs, and principles of American constitutional democracy.

- Knows how various American holidays reflect the shared values, principles, and beliefs of Americans.

Source: *Content Knowledge: A Compendium of Standards and Benchmarks for K–12 Education.* 4th edition. (Mid-continent Research for Education and Learning, 2004)

How to Use This Book

These booklets can be completed during class or as homework. Before students begin, walk them through each page so that they clearly understand how to respond to the writing prompts and how to read any challenging text features, such as charts or diagrams. If students need additional support, guide them as they work on a section of a booklet. You might have students complete a booklet over the course of several days, working on a few pages at a time.

Activate Prior Knowledge

Introduce each booklet with a discussion that activates students' prior knowledge. Ask students what they know about the topic, what they think they'll learn about the topic from the booklet, and what they would like to learn about the topic.

Walk Through the Booklet

After introducing the booklet and discussing the topic, walk through the pages together to satisfy children's curiosity and clarify the instructions. Point out the writing and drawing prompts and explain to students that although everyone is starting with the same booklet, they will each have a unique book when they are finished.

Read, Write, Draw, and Learn

Read and discuss the text together, pointing out vocabulary words and raising questions. Then move on to the accompanying writing and drawing prompts. Generate possible answers with students. Encourage students to write in complete sentences. Talk about what they learned from a particular section. Were they surprised about something they learned? Do they want to know more about a topic?

Share

At various points in the bookmaking process, have students share their written responses with their classmates. Draw attention to the similarities and differences in their responses. Be sure to send the booklets home for students to share with families. The repeated readings will help children develop fluency.

Extend Learning

On pages 7–8, you'll find two extension activities for each booklet. These will reinforce concepts covered in the books and explore a particular topic in more depth.

How to Assemble the Booklets

It works well to assemble the booklets together as a class.

Directions:

1. Carefully remove the perforated pages from the book.
2. Make double-sided copies of each page on standard 8½- by 11-inch paper.
3. Fold each page in half along the dashed line.
4. Place the pages in numerical order and staple along the spine.

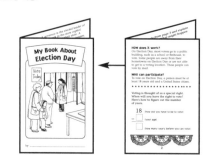

TIP: You may want to have students fill in their books before stapling them. This way the center pages will lie flat while students are writing.

Extension Activities

My Book About Election Day

- After explaining to students that a presidential inauguration is the swearing in to office of the president-elect, compile data to create a T-chart showing the age of several presidents at the time of their inauguration. Then analyze the data. Were any presidents the same age at inauguration? Who was the youngest inaugurated president on your list?

- Have students use their letters on page 7 of the booklet to inspire a poster that persuades reluctant Americans to vote. Discuss the written messages as well as the visuals that might convince people to vote.

My Book About Thanksgiving

- Invite students to create books about what they are thankful for. Have students fold two sheets of paper in half to create an eight-page book. On the cover, have students write, "I Am Thankful for . . ." On the first spread, students can write something they are thankful for on the left and draw an illustration on the right. Have students continue to fill in the rest of the spreads in the same way. On the back page, students can draw their Thanksgiving celebration.

- Students may be surprised to learn that the Harvest Feast of 1621 was not the first celebration for giving thanks. Native Americans held Thanksgiving celebrations long before Europeans arrived in America. In fact, the Wampanoag held several Thanksgiving festivals throughout the year. Have students research and share information about Native American Thanksgiving celebrations.

My Book About Winter Holidays

- Have students research other winter holidays. Invite them to add pages to their booklets with information about these holidays.

- Use the chart on pages 3 and 4 of the booklet as a jumping-off point for holiday research. Then have students select two holidays to compare and contrast in a Venn diagram.

My Book About New Year's Celebrations

- Invite students to make New Year's cards for the different traditions included in the booklet. Display these on a bulletin board with the title "Celebrating the New Year Around the World."

- Make a K-W-L chart. Before completing the booklets, have students share what they already know about all the New Year's traditions presented in the booklet. Create a chart for each New Year or divide one chart into three sections. Find out what else students want to know about each holiday. After completing the booklet, discuss what students learned.

My Book About Dr. Martin Luther King, Jr.

- Have students write five questions based on the timeline on pages 3 and 4 of the booklet, such as "How many years after Dr. King became a minister did he give his 'I Have a Dream' speech?" Students can then trade papers with a partner.

- Create a chart-size version of the timeline. Leave room for students to add new information as they learn about Dr. King.

My Book About Presidents' Day

- Display a picture of Mount Rushmore and share information about this national monument and the presidents featured on it. Visit www.nps.gov/moru for more information about Mount Rushmore.

- Create class books titled "If We Met George Washington" and "If We Met Abraham Lincoln." Have students share with the class what they wrote on pages 5 and 6 of the booklet. Then have students rewrite their responses on a larger sheet of paper and illustrate them on a separate sheet. Compile the written responses and illustrations to create two class books.

My Book About Earth Day

- Begin with a discussion of the word *pledge*. Then brainstorm things we as individuals can do to make Earth a safer place for all living things. What actions are students taking already? What new actions are they willing to take this year? Have students record and illustrate their pledges and then share them with their classmates.

- Create a collaborative Earth Day bulletin board based on the information in this book. You might include a large picture of Earth surrounded by what students learned about the importance of caring for our planet.

My Book About Memorial Day

- Invite students to write poems about Memorial Day. Encourage them to think about what they learned about this holiday and to focus their poem on one aspect of it.

- Make a Memorial Day word web. Write "Memorial Day" in the center of the web, and help students brainstorm words associated with this holiday, such as *war, peace, courage, soldier, flag, American, families, parade, remember,* and *honor.* Discuss the meaning of the words and how they relate to the holiday.

My Book About Flag Day

- The history of the holiday is presented as a sequence of events on pages 1 and 2 of this booklet. Discuss other ways to share the same information, such as on a timeline, in a date-event T-chart, or in a written paragraph. Help students realize that there are many ways to present the same information. Discuss the strengths of each format.

- Have students create a personal flag. Discuss the symbolism of the stars and stripes in the United States flag. Encourage students to design a flag that represents aspects of themselves—for example, they might use four hearts to show the number of people in their family or eight stripes to show their age.

My Book About the Fourth of July

- Review the timeline on pages 3 and 4 of the booklet. On chart paper, demonstrate how that information might look written in paragraph form. Explain that the paragraph needs to follow the same sequence as the timeline.

- Have students create their own multiple-choice quizzes similar to the one on page 2 of the booklet. Encourage them to ask questions about our nation's history. Have students take each other's quizzes and discuss the answers.

Selected References

Boynton, A. & Blevins, W. (2005). *Nonfiction passages with graphic organizers for independent practice: Grades 2–4.* New York: Scholastic.

Boynton, A. & Blevins, W. (2004). *Teaching students to read nonfiction: Grades 2–4.* New York: Scholastic.

Duke, N. K., & Bennett-Armistead, S. V. (2003). *Reading & writing informational text in the primary grades.* New York: Scholastic.

Kristo, J. V., & Bamford, R. A. (2004). *Nonfiction in focus.* New York: Scholastic.

My Book About Election Day

Vote Today

by _____

Voting Is Important

Did you know that only about 6 out of every 10 people who are able to vote actually do vote in a presidential election?

Write a letter to a person who chooses not to vote. Explain why each person's vote is important.

Dear American Citizen,

_____

_____

_____

_____

_____

Sincerely,

_____

7

All About Election Day

WHAT is it?

Election Day is the day when Americans elect, or choose through voting, their leaders. These leaders will run the government at the local, state, and national levels.

WHEN is it?

Election Day in this country is always the Tuesday after the first Monday in November.

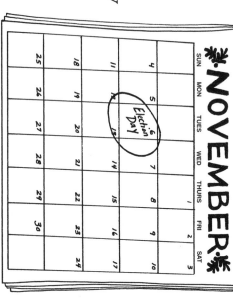

1

Governor: A governor is the elected leader of a state. Governors work in the state capitol building in the capital city of their state. A governor's job is to make sure that businesses, schools, transportation, and other things work well in the state.

Mayor: A mayor is the elected leader of a town or city. Mayors work in their town or city, sometimes in a building called City Hall. A mayor's job includes overseeing fire and police departments, schools, and libraries.

★ ★ ★ ★ ★ ★ ★ ★ ★ ★ ★ ★ ★ ★ ★

YOUR Community's Elected Leaders

Governor: _____

Mayor: _____

Senators: _____

and _____

Congressperson or Congresspeople: _____

_____

_____

6

HOW does it work?

On Election Day, most voters go to a public building, such as a school or firehouse, to vote. Some people are away from their hometowns on Election Day or are not able to get to a voting location. These people can vote by mail.

WHO can participate?

To vote on Election Day, a person must be at least 18 years old and a United States citizen.

★ ★ ★ ★ ★ ★ ★ ★ ★ ★ ★ ★ ★ ★ ★ ★ ★

Voting is thought of as a special right. When will you have the right to vote? Here's how to figure out the number of years.

18 (how old you have to be to vote)

— ☐ (your age)

‾‾‾‾

☐ (how many years before you can vote)

2

Our Elected Leaders

President: The president of the United States is our country's top elected leader. The president is elected every four years and lives and works in the White House in Washington, D.C. The president has many jobs, including signing laws, being in charge of the military, and meeting with other world leaders.

Senator: The United States Congress is responsible for making the country's laws. Congress is made up of two parts: the Senate and the House of Representatives. Each state elects two senators to the Senate. The president cannot make many important decisions without the advice and agreement of the Senate. Senators meet in the United States Capitol building in Washington, D.C.

Congressperson: Each state elects at least one congressperson to the House of Representatives. The total number elected depends on how many people live in that state. Congresspeople focus on writing the country's laws that have to do with money and taxes. Like senators, they meet in the United States Capitol in Washington, D.C.

5

Five Ways to Keep an Election Fair

1 Candidates (people running for a position or political office) and political parties (such as Democrats and Republicans) must be able to freely share information with the voters.

2 Any person who meets the requirements (such as age and citizenship) must be allowed to vote.

3 Any person who meets the requirements (such as age and citizenship) must be allowed to run for office.

4 People must be allowed to vote in private. This way, people will feel free to vote as they wish.

5 All votes must be counted fairly and correctly.

3

Choose one rule from page 3 and explain why it is important. What might happen if this rule did not exist?

_____

_____

Why is it necessary to have rules about voting?

_____

_____

_____

_____

_____

_____

_____

4

My Book About Thanksgiving

by ———

My Thanksgiving

Draw a picture of the family and friends you will spend Thanksgiving with this year. Write something that is special about the people in your picture.

7

The First Thanksgiving

Read the sequence of events below to learn about the Harvest Feast of 1621. This is sometimes called "the First Thanksgiving."

September 16, 1620
The Pilgrims set sail from England. They seek religious freedom in their new home.

November 11, 1620
After a difficult journey at sea, the Pilgrims land in Massachusetts.

Winter of 1620
Many Pilgrims do not survive the first hard winter.

Spring of 1621
With the help of a Native American named Squanto, the Pilgrims learn to farm and hunt food. Squanto was a Wampanoag.

Fall of 1621
The Pilgrims and about 90 Wampanoag share a feast to celebrate the successful harvest.

1

Squanto showed the Pilgrims the best places to catch fish.

He helped the Pilgrims and Native Americans communicate and trade with each other.

Without Squanto's help, the Pilgrim's story might have ended very differently. What do you think might have happened to the Pilgrims without Squanto?

6

In 1863, Abraham Lincoln made Thanksgiving a national holiday. On this day, we think about what we are thankful for.

Describe two things you are thankful for this year.

1. _____

_____

_____

2. _____

_____

2

Lending a Helping Hand

A Wampanoag named Squanto helped the Pilgrims survive in their new home.

Squanto helped the Pilgrims build warm homes.

He taught the Pilgrims to plant corn as soon as the leaves on the trees were the size of a squirrel's ears.

Squanto taught the Pilgrims how to grow corn. He told them to plant fish along with the corn. The fish **fertilizes** the soil, or makes it rich with nutrients. Rich soil helps the corn grow quickly.

5

The Harvest Feast

Look closely at the food on this Thanksgiving table. Put an X on four foods that the Pilgrims and Wampanoag would not have eaten. Remember, the Harvest Feast of 1621 celebrated the foods that the Pilgrims and Native Americans grew, caught, or prepared themselves.

hamburger

deer

pizza

turkey

soda

cabbage

pumpkin

beans

hot dog

bread

spinach

fish

carrots

duck

squash

Explain why you think these four foods were not eaten at the Harvest Feast of 1621.

Which foods that you eat on Thanksgiving are the **same as** or **similar to** those eaten at the Harvest Feast of 1621?

My Book About
Winter Holidays

by _____

Holiday Greetings

Create a greeting card for a holiday you celebrate. Think about the pictures and words you would like on your card. Then explain why you chose those pictures and words for your holiday card.

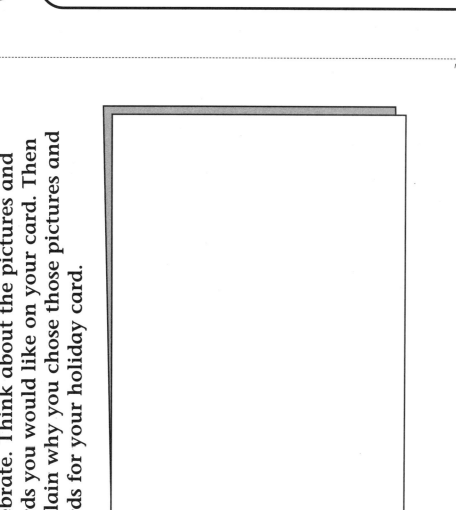

7

What the Holidays Are

Christmas celebrates the day that Jesus Christ was born. This is an important holiday for Christians around the world.

Hanukkah is also called the Festival of Lights. It celebrates a victory and a miracle. Long ago, Jewish warriors won a battle against the Syrians. Jewish people were again free to pray as they wished. When they took back their temple, they could find only enough oil to light the menorah for one day. The miracle is that the oil burned for eight days. That is why Hanukkah is celebrated for eight days.

This is something I learned about these holidays:

_____

_____

_____

_____

1

This is my favorite holiday tradition:

_____

_____

_____

This is a picture of my favorite holiday tradition:

6

All About

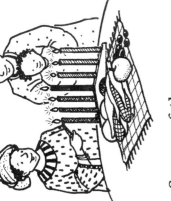
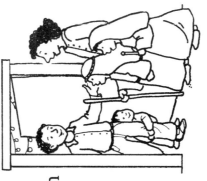

Kwanzaa celebrates the heritage of African Americans. The holiday is based on African harvest festivals. One of seven principles is remembered on each day of the holiday. Some of these principles are unity, creativity, and faith.

Las Posadas remembers Mary and Joseph's journey to Bethlehem and their search for shelter before Jesus was born. This nine-day-long holiday is part of Christmas celebrations in Mexico.

This is something I learned about these holidays:

_____

_____

2

My Winter Holiday

In the winter, I celebrate . . .

_____

This is how I help decorate my home:

_____

_____

_____

These are some of my favorite holiday foods:

_____

_____

_____

_____

5

Lights, Food, Fun!

Holiday	Lights	Special Foods	Fun
Christmas	People hang lights on bushes and Christmas trees.	Family and friends gather for a big meal. Christmas cookies and gingerbread houses are favorite sweets.	People exchange gifts and sing Christmas carols.
Hanukkah	People light candles in the menorah for eight nights.	Potato latkes with applesauce are a favorite treat.	Children play a dreidel game and win treats. People open presents and sing songs.
Kwanzaa	People light a candle in the kinara for each night of Kwanzaa.	Kwanzaa ends with a feast called the *karamu* that includes lots of fruits and vegetables.	People exchange handmade gifts called *zawadi* and tell stories.
Las Posadas	In some places, lights are strung on trees and buildings. People also hold candles as they gather to sing.	Sweets and fruits are given to children on each of the nine nights.	Families walk from house to house to reenact Mary and Joseph's search for shelter. They stop at a home for a party.

What is similar about these holidays?

What is different about these holidays?

Nonfiction Read & Write Booklets: Holidays Scholastic Teaching Resources

My Book About New Year's Celebrations

by _____

Try a New New Year's Tradition!

Draw a picture that shows you enjoying one of the New Year's traditions that you just learned about. Then describe what you are doing in your picture and why you chose that tradition.

7

Happy New Year!

New Year's Eve is celebrated on December 31—the evening before the first day of the New Year. Around the world, people gather with friends and family to celebrate the beginning of a new year.

Here are just a few traditions that welcome the New Year.

United States: People watch the celebration in New York City's Times Square on TV. As the ball drops, they count the last ten seconds until midnight. Then they cheer, blow noisemakers, and shout, "Happy New Year!"

Nonfiction Read & Write Booklets: Holidays Scholastic Teaching Resources

---

Lucky or Unlucky?

Chinese New Year traditions are often about bringing good luck for the New Year. Below is a list of lucky and unlucky objects and actions.

Lucky	Unlucky
• a clean house on New Year's Day	• using bad language during New Year's
• flowers that bloom inside the house on New Year's Day	• crying on New Year's Day means you will cry all year long
• "lucky money" is put in red envelopes with good luck messages on them and given to children	• an odd amount of "lucky money" because odd numbers are considered unlucky

Make up your own lucky or unlucky tradition and describe it below.

_____

_____

_____

_____

Spain: People listen as a large clock in Madrid strikes midnight. Then they eat 12 grapes—one at each of the 12 chimes.

Japan: At midnight, people begin to laugh. This is believed to bring good luck.

England: When a huge clock tower in London called Big Ben strikes midnight, people link arms and sing "Auld Lang Syne." These are Scottish words that mean "the good old days."

Describe similarities between these New Year's traditions.

_____

_____

2

Gung Hay Fat Choy!

This Chinese greeting means, "Have a prosperous (wealthy) and happy new year!" The Chinese New Year is a very important holiday in China and is celebrated by Chinese people all around the world. It takes place on different dates each year, between January 21 and February 20.

The New Year celebration lasts for 15 days. People have feasts, visit family and friends, and watch parades in which silk dragons and lions dance down the street.

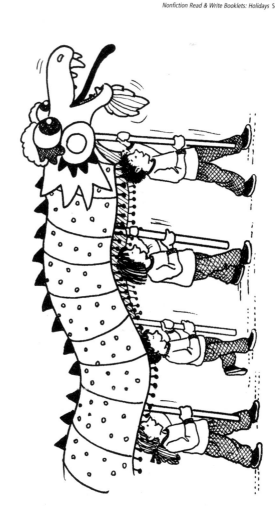

5

L'Shanah Tovah

This Hebrew greeting means "May it be a good and sweet year." These words are said at **Rosh Hashanah**, the Jewish New Year. Rosh Hashanah takes place in September or October. This is when the new year begins on the Jewish calendar.

Rosh Hashanah begins the ten days that are called the High Holy Days. At this time, Jewish people think about how they may have hurt friends and family over the past year. Then they ask those they have hurt for forgiveness. The High Holy Days end with **Yom Kippur.** On this day, people don't eat until sunset. This is meant to cleanse away their sins.

Bill, I'm sorry for borrowing your book without asking first.

That's okay, Greg. Thanks for telling me.

3

Rosh Hashanah Traditions

People eat apples dipped in honey to welcome a sweet year.

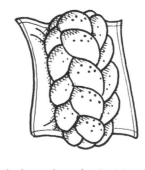

Challah (pronounced HA-la) is a type of bread that is usually shaped like a long braid. For Rosh Hashanah, the challah is baked round. A round challah stands for the circle of life.

The **shofar** is a ram's horn. It is blown 100 times during Rosh Hashanah to begin the High Holy Days.

Families and friends gather on Rosh Hashanah for a feast. The meal includes new fruits of the season, such as pomegranates.

4

My Book About
Dr. Martin Luther King, Jr.

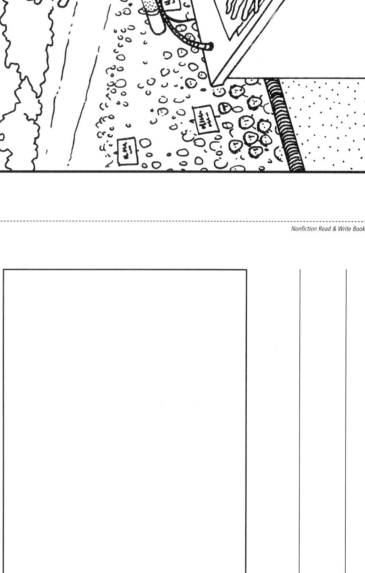

by _____

Dreams of Equality

Martin Luther King, Jr., dreamed of a day when all people would be treated equally. Thanks to his peaceful speeches, marches, and boycotts, our country is a better place.

Draw a picture that shows how you treat people with equality. Then describe your picture.

7

A Leader for Equality

Martin Luther King, Jr., lived from 1929 to 1968. He was an important leader for civil rights in the United States. During his lifetime, there were unfair laws that **segregated** people, or kept them apart. These laws were found mostly in southern states.

Under these laws, African-American people and white people could not go to the same restaurants, schools, or playgrounds. There was even a law that said that African Americans had to sit at the back of a bus, while white people sat in the front.

Civil rights are the rights to have freedom and be treated equally. How were African Americans denied their civil rights during Dr. King's lifetime?

1

Use your own words to explain what the quotation on page 5 means.

_____

_____

_____

Think about what you've read about Martin Luther King, Jr. Write four words or phrases that describe this great leader.

1.

2.

3.

4.

6

Martin Luther King, Jr., studied peaceful ways to end the unfair laws. One day in Montgomery, Alabama, a woman named Rosa Parks refused to give up her bus seat to a white person. She was arrested.

In response, Dr. King led a bus **boycott**. He thought that if African Americans stopped riding the bus, the bus company would have to change the rules. For 381 days, most African Americans stopped riding the bus in Montgomery. The Supreme Court finally decided that people riding the bus had the right to sit where they wanted.

Dr. King spent the rest of his life peacefully standing up for people's civil rights.

Why do you think the bus boycott was important?

_____

_____

_____

2

Words to Remember

"I have a dream that my four little children will one day live in a nation where they will not be judged by the color of their skin but by the content of their character."

—*Martin Luther King, Jr.*
August 28, 1963

Word	What It Means in This Quote
judged	formed an opinion about someone or something
content	what is contained in something
character	the qualities that make a person or thing what it is

5

The Life of a Leader

Martin Luther King, Jr., is born in Atlanta, Georgia.

He becomes a pastor at a church.

At Boston University, he earns a doctorate degree (the highest university degree).

He marries Coretta Scott.

He leads the Montgomery Bus Boycott in Alabama.

1920 1930 1940 1950 1960 1970 1980 1990

He gives his "I Have a Dream" speech in Washington, D.C.

He is killed in Tennessee.

He is given an important award for his work called the Nobel Peace Prize.

The Civil Rights Act is passed. This law gives African Americans more rights and protection.

Martin Luther King, Jr., Day becomes a national holiday on the third Monday in January.

Dr. King was the youngest person to receive the Nobel Peace Prize.

How old was he at that time? _____

How did you use the timeline to find the answer?

_____

The Nobel Peace Prize is awarded to someone who has done outstanding work for peace.

Why do you think Martin Luther King, Jr., was awarded this prize?

_____

Nonfiction Read & Write Booklets: Holidays Scholastic Teaching Resources

My Book About Presidents' Day

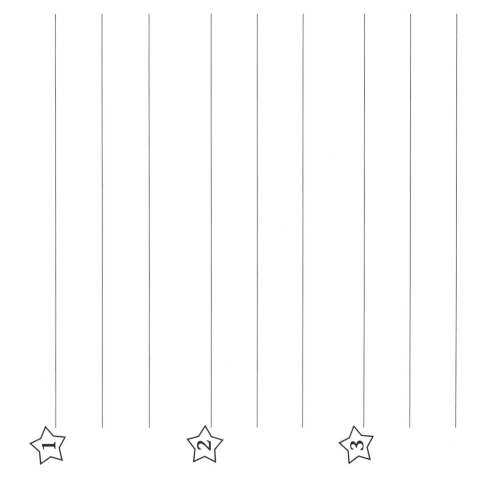

by _____

President

_____ (write your last name here)

Now imagine that **you** are the president of the United States of America! Write three things you would do to make our country a better place to live.

☆1 _____
_____
_____

☆2 _____
_____
_____

☆3 _____
_____
_____

7

Remembering Our Former Presidents

Presidents' Day first began as two separate holidays to celebrate the birthdays of George Washington and Abraham Lincoln. Both of these presidents were born in February. Today Presidents' Day honors the accomplishments of all former United States presidents. It takes place on the third Monday in February.

Read about some former United States presidents on the next page. Write three things you either know or would like to know about some of these or other former presidents.

1. _____
   _____

2. _____
   _____

3. _____
   _____

Abraham Lincoln is also known as "Honest Abe." It is said that when he was a young man working at a store, a woman once overpaid him six cents. What did Abe do? He walked three miles to the woman's house and returned the money.

Imagine that you lived at the same time as Abraham Lincoln. What would you say to him or ask him?

1. _____
   _____

2. _____
   _____

3. _____
   _____

Some Former Presidents

Name	Number of Presidency	Years in Office
John Adams	2nd president	1797–1801
Thomas Jefferson	3rd president	1801–1809
Ulysses S. Grant	18th president	1869–1877
Theodore Roosevelt	26th president	1901–1909
Woodrow Wilson	28th president	1913–1921
Calvin Coolidge	30th president	1923–1929
Franklin Delano Roosevelt	32nd president	1933–1945
John Fitzgerald Kennedy	35th president	1961–1963
Ronald Reagan	40th president	1981–1989
William Jefferson Clinton	42nd president	1993–2001

2

You May Also Know Them as . . .

George Washington is also known as the "Father of Our Country" because he was the first United States president and helped create the country's first laws.

Imagine that you lived at the same time as George Washington. What would you say to him or ask him?

_____

_____

_____

_____

_____

_____

_____

_____

5

Comparing Two Presidents

In the center of the Venn diagram, write ways that these two presidents are similar.

George Washington

- our nation's 1st president
- born February 22
- grew up in Virginia
- liked to ride horses, swim, and help with the family farm as a child
- led our country to victory against England in the Revolutionary War
- his face is on the one-dollar bill and the quarter

Both Presidents

- _____
- _____
- _____

Abraham Lincoln

- our nation's 16th president
- born February 12
- grew up in Kentucky and Indiana
- liked to read, tell jokes, and race other kids as a child
- led the North to victory against the South in the Civil War
- his face is on the five-dollar bill and the penny

My Book About Earth Day

by _____

Pitch In!

Draw a picture that shows you doing something to help Earth. Then describe how you are helping our planet in the picture.

_____

_____

_____

_____

7

The Man Who Began Earth Day

Gaylord Nelson was always interested in the environment, even as a boy. When he grew up, he became a **senator**. A senator is someone who helps make laws in our country. Nelson worked to write laws to protect the environment. The laws helped, but he wanted to do more.

He had an idea. Why not have a day on which people learn about Earth's problems and work on solutions? More than 20 million people from across the country took part in the first Earth Day on April 22, 1970. Today, people all over the world make promises to help our planet on Earth Day.

Thank you, Gaylord Nelson, for helping us see that Earth needs our attention and help!

1

Choose an endangered or threatened animal to research. Complete the chart with the information you learned about this animal.

Draw your animal here.

Animal: _____

6

Problem-Solution Chart

What are some of the problems in our environment? What are some possible solutions? Fill in the chart below.

Problem	Possible Solution
1. People use a lot of gas to drive their cars. This pollutes the air.	1. People can carpool or take the bus so that there are fewer cars on the road. They can also walk to places that are nearby.
2.	2.
3.	3.

2

You Can Help

When we protect the environment, we also protect animals' habitats. Some of these animals are endangered or threatened.

Animal	Bengal Tiger	Bald Eagle
Where is the animal's habitat?	Bengal tigers live in grasslands, shrublands, rain forests, and mangroves in India, Nepal, and Southeast Asia.	Bald eagles build nests on edges of rivers, lakes, and seashores, and along high peaks in North America.
Why is the animal endangered or threatened?	People kill tigers for their fur and use the tigers' fat and crushed bones to make medicine.	A farm chemical called DDT made fish sick. Eagles ate the fish. The DDT made their eggs soft. Few babies hatched.
How is the animal being protected?	Reserves and conservation programs protect tigers. The government of Nepal tags tigers to keep track of them.	In 1972, DDT was banned. Zoos also began to breed bald eagles and release them into the wild.

5

Nonfiction Read & Write Booklets: Holidays Scholastic Teaching Resources

How Rain Forests Help the World

- More than half of the world's animal species live in the rain forest.

- Almost half of all the medicines we use come from the rain forest.

- Rain forests take in huge amounts of carbon dioxide (a poisonous gas). Through **photosynthesis**, leaves on plants and trees change carbon dioxide into oxygen that we breathe.

How People Harm the Rain Forest

- Logging companies cut down too many trees. As a result, animals lose their homes.

- Cattle ranchers clear land to raise cattle. When the cattle destroy the land, the ranchers move on to new land.

- Many tourists visit rain forests, leading people to cut down trees to make room for roads and hotels. This also causes more pollution.

Imagine you are writing a letter to someone who doesn't think the rain forest is important. In your letter, explain why we need to preserve the rain forest.

Dear _____,

_____

_____

_____

_____

_____

Sincerely,

_____

Nonfiction Read & Write Booklets: Holidays Scholastic Teaching Resources

My Book About Memorial Day

by _____

Freedom!

Countries often fight wars to protect their freedom, protect the freedom of others, or win freedom from another country. In the United States, we have many freedoms, such as the freedom to say and write what we think and to vote for our leaders.

Below, describe freedoms that you and your family enjoy. In what ways is freedom important to you?

_____

_____

_____

_____

_____

_____

_____

7

Remembering Our Heroes

Memorial Day falls on the last Monday in May. On this holiday, many people celebrate the beginning of summer with picnics and outdoor fun. But Memorial Day is serious, too. On this holiday, we remember the men and women in the American armed forces who died in war.

Memorial Day began a long time ago, after the Civil War ended. The Civil War took place between 1861 and 1865. In the Civil War, the northern and southern states fought each other, and many soldiers were killed. People wanted to remember the soldiers who had died.

Read the timeline on page 2 to learn how Memorial Day came to be.

1

If you were to design a memorial, what would it look like and whom or what would it honor?

Describe your memorial below.

6

Memorial Day Timeline

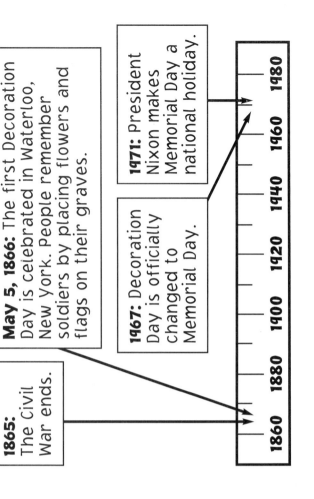

1865: The Civil War ends.

May 5, 1866: The first Decoration Day is celebrated in Waterloo, New York. People remember soldiers by placing flowers and flags on their graves.

1967: Decoration Day is officially changed to Memorial Day.

1971: President Nixon makes Memorial Day a national holiday.

1860 1880 1900 1920 1940 1960 1980

What words of gratitude, or thankfulness, would you share with those who have served our country in the military?

2

Our Memorials

A memorial is built to remind people of an important person, group, or event. Below are just a few memorials that honor our soldiers.

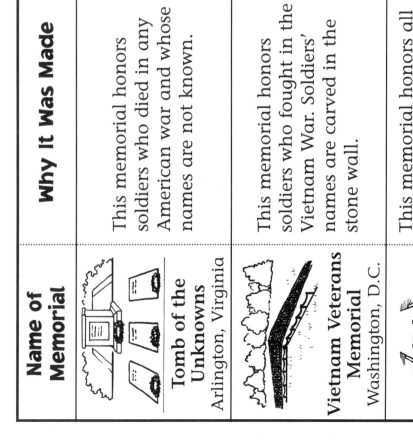

Name of Memorial	Why It Was Made
Tomb of the Unknowns Arlington, Virginia	This memorial honors soldiers who died in any American war and whose names are not known.
Vietnam Veterans Memorial Washington, D.C.	This memorial honors soldiers who fought in the Vietnam War. Soldiers' names are carved in the stone wall.
National World War II Memorial Washington, D.C.	This memorial honors all who served during World War II—the soldiers who died, the veterans, and the sacrifice and spirit of Americans at home who supported the war.

5

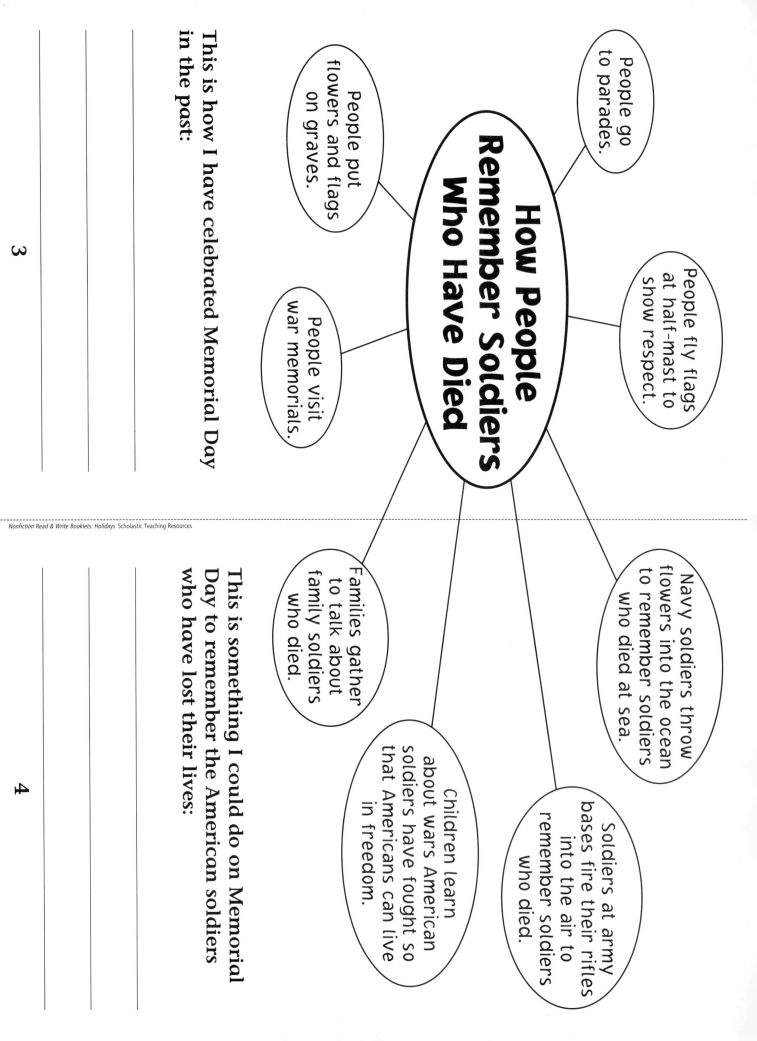

How People Remember Soldiers Who Have Died

People go to parades.

People fly flags at half-mast to show respect.

People put flowers and flags on graves.

People visit war memorials.

Navy soldiers throw flowers into the ocean to remember soldiers who died at sea.

Soldiers at army bases fire their rifles into the air to remember soldiers who died.

Children learn about wars American soldiers have fought so that Americans can live in freedom.

Families gather to talk about family soldiers who died.

This is how I have celebrated Memorial Day in the past:

3

This is something I could do on Memorial Day to remember the American soldiers who have lost their lives:

4

My Book About Flag Day

Flag Day—June 14th

by _____

The American Flag and You

The American flag is an important symbol of our country. It stands for many American ideals, such as freedom, hope, equality, individuality, and justice.

Use the letters in the word *flag* to write an acrostic poem that describes what the American flag means to you.

The letters *f*, *l*, *a*, and *g* may be the first letter of each line of the poem, or they may appear in the middle of a sentence or word.

F _____

L _____

A _____

G _____

7

The Story of Flag Day

Americans celebrate Flag Day on June 14. Read about the history behind this holiday.

1775

The United States was not a country at this time. There were 13 colonies in North America that were ruled by England. The colonists no longer wanted to be ruled by England and unfairly taxed by King George III. To win their freedom, they went to war against England. The Revolutionary War began on April 19, 1775.

JULY 4, 1776

The Declaration of Independence was signed. Written by Thomas Jefferson, this document announced to the world that "These United Colonies" were "Free and Independent States." The United States declared that it was free from England's rule, but the war continued.

JUNE 14, 1777

George Washington and other American leaders felt the United States needed a flag. They chose a design that included a star and stripe for each of the 13 colonies. On June 14, 1777, this design became official.

Nonfiction Read & Write Booklets: Holidays Scholastic Teaching Resources

Betsy Ross told George Washington that she thought the stars would be better with five points rather than six. She also thought the flag would fly better in the wind if it were a rectangle instead of a square. George Washington and the other men approved of her plan and asked her to sew the first flag.

Why do you think people continue to tell the story of Betsy Ross?

_____

_____

_____

_____

_____

_____

_____

1885

A Wisconsin schoolteacher named B. J. Cigrand had an idea to celebrate the flag's birthday. Many magazine and newspaper articles were written about his idea, and Flag Day celebrations spread across the country.

1949

President Truman made Flag Day a national holiday.

Do you think it's important to celebrate Flag Day? Why or why not?

2

Who Was Betsy Ross?

Some people think that Betsy Ross made the first American flag. But many experts agree that we can't prove that this actually happened. Even so, the story of Betsy Ross continues to be told. This is her story.

Betsy Ross was a seamstress. She worked out of her shop near the Pennsylvania State House. One day in 1776, George Washington and two other leaders came to her shop. They showed her a drawing of a flag and asked if she could make it.

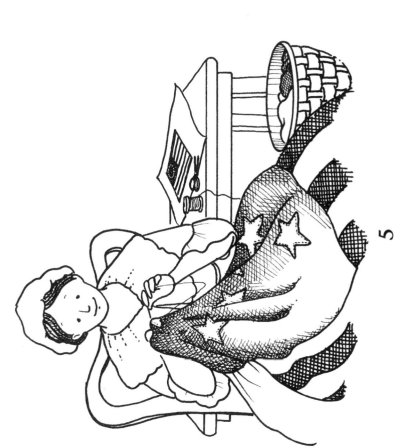

5

Our First Flag

The 13 white stars stand for the 13 original colonies. The stars are in a circle so that no one colony would be viewed as more important than another.

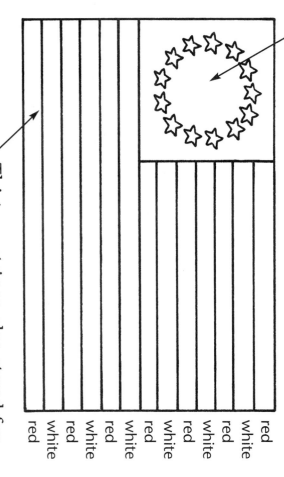

Thirteen stripes also stand for the 13 original colonies. The stripes are red and white.

How are the two flags the same?

_____

_____

_____

3

Our Flag Today

As more states were added to the union, more stars were added to the flag. Today's flag has 50 stars—one for each state.

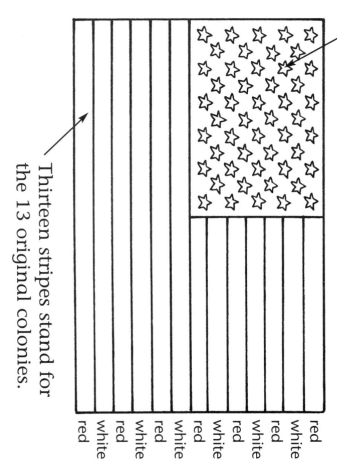

Thirteen stripes stand for the 13 original colonies.

How are the two flags different?

_____

_____

_____

4

My Book About the Fourth of July

by _____

Let's Celebrate!

Draw a picture of how you might celebrate this Fourth of July. Then describe what is happening in your picture.

7

Independence Day

The Fourth of July is also known as Independence Day. To be **independent** means:

• To be able to take care of your own needs
• To make your own rules
• Not to be under the control or rule of another
• Not to be connected with anyone or anything else

1

Who Wrote the Declaration?

Congress chose a five-person committee, or group, to write the document. The committee asked Thomas Jefferson to create a draft. He summarized the important beliefs and ideas of the colonists. The people who signed the Declaration of Independence put their lives in danger. Writing something against the British government was a crime!

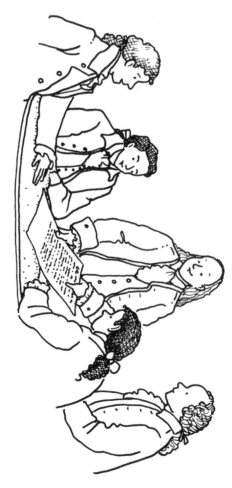

Think about all you learned about the colonists and their fight for independence. Write four words that describe the colonists.

_____

_____

_____

_____

6

Do you know how our country gained independence, and from whom? Take this quiz. Then check your answers on the timeline on the following pages.

1. Where did the Pilgrims come from?
   ○ France   ○ England   ○ Spain

2. How many original colonies were there?
   ○ 13   ○ 50   ○ 5

3. Why were the colonists angry with the British?
   ○ The British demanded that the colonists return to England to live.
   ○ The British ignored the colonists and didn't offer them any help.
   ○ The British taxed the colonists on everyday goods and did not let them rule themselves.

4. Who led the colonial army in the war against the British?
   ○ Samuel Adams
   ○ George Washington
   ○ Abraham Lincoln

2

What Is the Declaration of Independence?

The Declaration of Independence is a document written by the colonists. In it, they announced to England that they would govern themselves. The Declaration of Independence also describes a new government that had never been tried before—a government that gets its power from the people it governs.

IN CONGRESS   July 4 1776
The unanimous Declaration of the thirteen United States of America

5

A Nation Is Born

In 1620, Pilgrims left England to seek religious freedom. They made their home in Massachusetts. Over the years, 13 colonies were established along the east coast. These colonies were ruled by England. What happened next?

1767: England puts a tax (or fee) on imported goods such as tea, paper, and glass. The colonists protest by not buying these items.

1768: British troops arrive in Boston to stop the colonists from giving the British authorities a hard time.

1772: Samuel Adams forms a committee in Boston to organize the colonies' protest against the British.

1773: In an act of rebellion, colonists dress as Native Americans, walk onto a British ship, and throw 342 chests of tea into Boston Harbor. This is known as the Boston Tea Party.

April 19, 1775: The Revolutionary War begins with the battles of Lexington and Concord.

June 15, 1775: George Washington is chosen to lead the colonists in the war against England.

July 4, 1776: The Declaration of Independence is signed, stating that the colonies are free from England.

1781: The British surrender.

1760   1765   1770   1775   1780   1785

Write something you learned about how our country became an independent nation.

Nonfiction Read & Write Booklets: Holidays Scholastic Teaching Resources